D1555732

# BASIC BUDDHISM

# FOR A

# WORLD IN TROUBLE

## BRIAN TAYLOR

www.universaloctopus.com

Other Publications in the
BASIC BUDDHISM SERIES

What is Buddhism?
Buddhism and Drugs
The Five Buddhist Precepts
Basic Buddhist Meditation
The Living Waters of Buddhism
The Ten Fetters (*Sanjojana*)
The Five Nivaranas *(Buddha's Teaching
of the Five Hindrances*)
Dependent Origination (*Paṭiccasamuppāda*)
Buddhist Pali Chants with English Translations

Published by Universal Octopus 2016
www.universaloctopus.com

A catalogue record of this book is available from the
British Library.

ISBN 978-0-9571901-3-9

# CONTENTS

# INTRODUCTION

A world in trouble?

War in the Far East and the Middle East. Suicide bombers. Riots on the streets. Gaols and Psychiatric hospitals full. Soaring crime. Racial hatred. Violence in the schools and in the home. Economic Meltdown.

Yes. A world in trouble.

Everywhere man is striving for Freedom. But he understands freedom as freedom to do what he wants. But a man who does what he wants is often not free at all. He is the slave of his desires. Real freedom is not freedom *to* but freedom *from*.

Freedom from suffering.

Here is the answer. Simple, straightforward. Open to any man whatever his background.

## THE QUIET MIND

The Sun
shines
in a bucket of water
but doesn't
get wet.

# 1. **WHAT IS BUDDHISM?**

B uddhism is a method by which one can put an end to the suffering that we experience in this world.

'Suffering' means all those experiences, large and small, which have characteristics that we do not want. Experiences that are painful, unpleasant, tiresome, frustrating, irritating or depressing.

Birth is suffering. Sickness is suffering. Old age is suffering. Death is suffering. Not having what we want is suffering. Having to put up with what we do not want is suffering.

Suffering is experienced through the six sense doors. Bodily suffering is felt when the sense of touch comes into contact with a disagreeable sense object, some-thing hot or sharp or pressing. It also occurs when the more sensitive organs of touch, the eye, the ear, the nose and the tongue, come into contact with stimuli to which they are vulnerable. The eye is affected by light, the ear by sound waves, the nose by gases and particles and the tongue by objects of taste. The mind organ also experiences suffering by way of states of mind and thoughts: regret, remorse, anger, envy, worry, restlessness, jealousy, despair, loneliness, desire.

Apart from these six senses, no suffering is experienced, since it is through the senses that sense objects are contacted and experience takes place. Without these senses there would be no experience at all and no suffering.

Without our senses the world would not exist for us.

According to Buddhism, things occur because there is a cause for them: a footprint needs a foot; warmth requires a source of heat and so on. Few would deny this, but in Buddhism it is taken further and applied universally. Death occurs because there is Birth. Birth occurs because there is a desire to be born.

Suffering, too, does not occur spontaneously. It also has a cause. The cause of suffering is the grasping out through the six senses at the objects of sense and the clinging to them. If we did not do this we would not suffer. Consider the analogy of the red-hot poker. If we grasp after it and cling to it, our hand is burned and we suffer.

Conversely, if the cause is removed, then the effect will cease. No foot, no footprint. No birth, no death. If we let go of the poker and no longer grasp after it, our wounds will heal in due course and after that there will be no more pain. Why does one grasp out through the six senses at the sense objects that make up the experiences of life?

Because one considers them desirable. One wants to be born. One wants the poker. This strong desire clouds one's judgement so that one is unable to see the other side of things. The consequences. Being born means sickness, old age and death. Grasping the poker means being burned. Buddhism attempts to tell us (or remind us) that the state of *not* grasping out through the senses at sense objects is an absolute, eternal state of pure peace and happiness and it calls this state Nibbāna.

It is not Death, as those who believe there is only one life understand. Nibbāna is like a cinema screen. The universe is all the pictures and images superimposed on the screen. Because of the pictures, we can't see the screen. Yet it is there all the time. If we could clear the screen of the pictures, we would see it immediately. If we could stop all sense perceptions and thoughts and images, Nibbāna would be revealed.

When we find the whole universe, mind and body, unsatisfactory, and let them go, they fall away from us and we experience total Peace and Happiness. This is a state that has always been there. From time to time we get flashes of it. It is not death. Death is the end of something. Nibbāna is not the end of anything. It is a state without a beginning and without an end.

Buddhism also lays down a method, a way of behaving and acting in everyday life, which is designed to lead human beings, step by step, to a personal realisation of the state of Nibbāna. The Buddha introduced this method over 2,500 years ago and it still exists in its original form. Even today, men and women who conscientiously put it into actual practice are able to put an end to suffering and reach Nibbāna.

## 2. **THE LIVING WATERS OF BUDDHISM**

Turn on the tap. Out comes water. Mix it with tea leaves and call it Tea. Mix it with coffee grains and call it Coffee. Mix it with fermented hops and call it Beer. Mix it with coloured pigments and call it Paint. Mix it with arsenic and call it Poison.

Water is cool, refreshing and necessary to sustain life. But what is mixed with it can change its nature, making it not cool, not refreshing, even inimical to life. It can be made to stimulate, inflame or even kill.

Buddhism is the cool water of the universe. It is refreshing. It sustains the holy life. It revives the parched heart of man.

But as it flows from its fountainhead in Bodhi Gaya, it becomes mixed with other things. It becomes Mahayana, Theravada, Yogacara, Soto, Zen. It is mixed with national and racial characteristics. There is Indian Buddhism, Thai Buddhism, Ceylonese Buddhism, Japanese Buddhism, Chinese Buddhism, Tibetan Buddhism. Even American and English Buddhism.

It also gets mixed with cultural and aesthetic additives. You find Buddhist painting, Buddhist literature, Buddhist sculpture, Buddhist iconography, Buddhist drama, Buddhist poetry.

It has even been mixed with martial arts. Martial arts kill.

Many of these national and cultural flowerings of Buddhism are of interest in their own right. They tell us a great deal about the peoples and societies that have produced them. But it is sometimes difficult to discern the living water of Buddhism itself. Just as it is difficult to distinguish the distinctive qualities of water in, say, a glass of whisky which is fiery, burning, intoxicating and parches the palate.

With water you refer back to the basic structure of water. Two parts Hydrogen. One part Oxygen. Every-thing else, whatever its merits, is not water. With Buddhism it is the same. What are the basic teachings of Buddha himself? Not Guru This or Acharn That.

Fortunately, the Buddha's teachings have been very well preserved in the language that he spoke himself. The Pali Language has been thoroughly investigated and explained by many fine scholars in different cultures over a long period. Although there will always be different opinions as to how best to translate some of the Buddha's concepts into different modern languages, there is general agreement as to what these concepts mean.

In addition, although the Buddha touched on different subjects and used a variety of images to illustrate what he was saying, the main themes are repeated again and again in sutta[1] after sutta. Even the same logical sequences, which link these themes in an organised whole, are continually restated in sutta after sutta.

To what effect? The Buddha begins with the unsatisfactoriness of Life as living beings actually experience it. He then demonstrates what the cause of this unsatisfactoriness is. Then he indicates that there is a state of Total Freedom and Happiness, which is permanent and unchanging. Finally, and most important of all for those of us who wish to do something about our predicament, he outlines a simple step-by-step method by which the state of perfection can be reached by any sincere and normal human being.

The living water of Buddhism is this method, which quenches the thirst of a suffering world.

---

[1] Sutta: *A discourse given by the Buddha or one of his senior disciples.*

The other things which have accrued to Buddhism – artistic, cultural, ceremonial, philosophical, nationalist additions – may well have great merit in themselves but they are not Buddhism and they need to be clearly distinguished from Buddhism. To the anthropologist this may not be important. He takes things as he finds them and as they have developed.

But for the practitioner who wishes to do what the Buddha says should be done for one's own welfare, it is essential to be clear about the basic Buddhism that the Buddha actually taught. It was to liberate beings, not to educate them in other ways, that the Buddha arose from his Samādhi[2].

As is stated in the Majjhima–Nikāya (The Middle Length Sayings), Sutta 29:

*"THE PURPOSE OF THE HOLY LIFE DOES NOT CONSIST IN ACQUIRING ALMS, HONOUR, OR FAME, NOR IN GAINING MORALITY, CONCENTRATION, OR KNOWLEDGE AND VISION. THE OBJECT OF THE HOLY LIFE, ITS ESSENCE, ITS GOAL IS UNSHAKEABLE LIBERATION OF MIND."*

It is necessary from the outset to be clear in one's own mind that one wants this "liberation of mind". A man drinks whisky not to quench

---

2 Samādhi: *State of Perfect Peace and Calm*.

his thirst but to enflame his senses. He drinks not for the water itself but for the alcohol for which the water is just a carrying agent.

Similarly a man can study Buddhist art because he is interested in art. He can study the Pali language because he is interested in languages or poetry or history. If he does this he will not become liberated, nor will he want to be. Just as the drinker of whisky will not have his thirst quenched, nor will he want this.

But a man who does want to be liberated will seek out the pure essence of Buddhism just as a thirsty man will seek pure water. And the pure essence of Buddhism presents a method for achieving, once and for all, this "unshakeable liberation of mind". It is compared to cool, living water because the opposite of liberation is bondage. Bondage, as far as the mind is concerned, has the characteristic of heat and passion. Heat and passion accompany grasping after experience and sensation. The world, said the Buddha, is on fire, burning. Burning with craving, anger, hatred, envy, frustration, excitement, fear, remorse, disappointment. We can see this for ourselves. To be free from this, we need to liberate ourselves.

Liberate ourselves from what? From craving.

Why craving?

Because it is craving which causes suffering in all its many forms by leading a man to grasp after the objects of his desires. And the objects of his craving invariably betray him. What are the objects of this craving? They are all the various phenomena of life itself. Things that are seen or heard or smelt or tasted or touched with this human body. And the human body itself, which is known by seeing, hearing, smelling, tasting and feeling. The whole physical universe is our body and the extensions of our body. Without our bodies we would have no access to the physical universe and it would not exist for us.

Mental Objects, too, are objects of this craving. Thoughts, feelings, memories and imagination make up the mental universe and we use our minds to contact them. Without our minds we would have no access to this mental universe and it would not exist for us.

We have this body and this mind. They are constantly inter-reacting by way of cause and effect. Together they are the objects of this craving. We grasp after all the paraphernalia that make up mind and body, continually, incessantly, from moment to moment. And because we do this we put ourselves at the mercy of these things.

And we suffer. We do not find satisfaction in these things. We see things and they are unpleasant, so we experience dissatisfaction. We see pleasant things and they do not last, so we experience dissatisfaction. We see neutral things and we find them of no interest to us, so we experience dissatisfaction. And this same pattern of dissatisfaction is experienced through the ear, the nose, the mouth and the sense of touch. And the mind. Moment to moment. Day and night. Month after month. Year after year. Lifetime after lifetime. There is no end to the flow of phenomena.

The actual objects of our senses are not within our ultimate control. Nor are the senses themselves. We cannot make our eyes and ears last forever. We cannot ensure that pleasant experiences will occur when we want them to and last for as long as we want. We cannot ensure that we will remain free of unpleasant experiences. We cannot say, "*I choose not to be sick. Not to grow old. Not to die.*" So long as we are in contact with phenomena, we cannot be free of them.

We remain in contact with them because there is a grasping after them. Freedom comes when this grasping is replaced by a letting go. A letting go of the objects of sense and the objects of mind.

Control of these things is not within our power. "Unshakeable Liberation" from them is. We cannot prevent fire from burning our hands by telling it to be cool. Because the nature of fire is not to be cool. *But we can prevent our hands from reaching out and grasping after the fire.*

> *"THE PURPOSE OF THE HOLY LIFE DOES NOT CONSIST IN ACQUIRING ALMS, HONOUR, OR FAME, NOR IN GAINING MORALITY, CONCENTRATION, OR KNOWLEDGE AND VISION. THE OBJECT OF THE HOLY LIFE, ITS ESSENCE, ITS GOAL IS UNSHAKEABLE LIBERATION OF MIND."*

Pure water is hydrogen and oxygen. Nothing more. Pure Buddhism is the path to Liberation. Nothing more. A man who sees this clearly rouses himself and makes straight for his Eternal Home, Nibbāna. Buddhism is straightforward and direct. It teaches cause and effect. Do this and that will result. Avoid this and that will cease.

What is of the utmost importance is to grasp the fact that, if the Buddha's instructions are scrupulously and honestly followed, the attainment of Nibbāna is assured for any human being who is reading this passage here and now.

If one deviates from the clear instructions, the goal is no longer assured. If one doesn't follow the map, one may end up somewhere else. If one is half-hearted, if one changes the rules to fit in with Thai customs, English customs, American customs, Tibetan customs, Japanese customs, Chinese customs, the goal is no longer assured. If one attempts to blend Buddhism with modern Science, with contemporary ideas, with politics, with sociology, the goal is no longer assured.

Pure Buddhism is direct and clear. Do this, achieve that.

Do what?

The Buddha has told us how to walk, how to stand, how to sit and how to lie down. We are told to do all these mindfully and with clear comprehension. He has told us how to eat, how to attend to the needs of the body.

Mindfully.

He has told us how to speak: honestly, straight-forwardly and without harsh language, slander, gossip or vain talk.

He has told us how to behave in our dealings with the world and with others. We should not kill, or steal, or betray our wives and husbands, or lie and deceive. We should avoid alcohol and drugs because they cause carelessness and carelessness leads to suffering for ourselves and others.

He has told us how to earn a living. We should support ourselves in ways which are honest and do not cause suffering. We should not trade in living beings, or weapons. We should not be butchers. We should not sell alcohol or intoxicating drugs or poisons. We should support the Order of Monks and the Buddha's Teaching.

He has told us how to think. We should empty our minds of negative and unprofitable thoughts.

We should develop positive states of mind; compassion, friendliness, diligence, detachment, patience, generosity, perseverance. We should develop understanding and wisdom.

He has told us that right understanding means seeing that life is not chaotic or random in the way it works but proceeds by cause and effect, which he calls Karma.

Karma means "doing", "action". Its opposite is not doing, no action.

Everything which is done, proceeds by cause and effect. I drop the cup, it breaks. I press the switch, the light comes on.

Nothing is random. If I sow carrot seeds, I get carrots. I don't get parsnips. If I press the wall next to the switch, the light doesn't come on.

All around us in the world and inside us in our minds, what we see are the effects of innumerable causes. The houses we live in, the people we associate with, environmental problems, the clothes we wear, the thoughts and memories we have, our ideas and opinions, our physical fitness. We can recognise a lot of this.

Buddhism takes it further and says, *all* phenomena are the results of causes.

But the effects of causes are also the causes of future effects. I make a sculpture. From this I make a mould. The mould is used to make more sculptures. The carrots grow; their seeds will produce more carrots. My thoughts are the cause of more thoughts, or words, or actions. Cause and effect are two aspects of the same thing seen at different points in time.

This is Karma.

It is important in the realm of ethics. Just as a good seed produces a good plant, so a good deed means a good result.

*The Law is mirror-like in its precision*
*and its simplicity needs no revision;*
*that Good breeds Good*
*and Evil has its price;*
*that Virtue is its own reward.*
*And so is Vice.*

Those who cannot see the connection between cause and effect are often too hasty. Like the small boy who, hearing that an acorn would grow into an oak tree, planted his acorn and came back a week later looking for his oak tree. *"It doesn't work,"* he said.

*It is easier to chop down*
*an acorn*
*than an oak.*

*(The branch you bang*
*your head on*
*is an acorn*
*that you missed.)*

Here and now we are surrounded by a world of effects. Here and now everything we think and say and do acts as a cause and will produce corresponding effects. We are free to choose. We have inherited the past. We can create a future we would like to inherit. Starting with our own thoughts and intentions.

Fundamental to this process is; do good, get good; do bad, get bad.

Right understanding also means seeing that things have three fundamental characteristics: *unsatisfactoriness, impermanence* and *having nothing in it which is ourselves or belongs to us.*

It means seeing that if we continue to grasp after things which we cannot control and which let us down, we cannot realise and experience Nibbāna, the eternal, peaceful state, which is the end of all suffering.

Buddha has provided us with a straightforward method by which we can train our minds to realise Nibbāna ourselves – Insight Meditation.

What we have to do is put it all into practice for ourselves. Without delay. For the mind that is reading this at this moment does not know how much longer his or her life will last.

This is the pure water of Buddhism; the message of Liberation and the Path leading to it.

Anything else, the statues, the incense, the pictures, the costumes, the ceremonies, the fortune-telling, the adaptations to suit different cultural and national backgrounds, the involvement in politics or social welfare, or linguistic studies -

all these are of great interest to the student of life, but they are not pure Buddhism.

Pure Buddhism is the Living Water of the Universe.

Who will drink it?

# 3. **GETTING STARTED**

The emphasis in Buddhism is always on identifying the *cause* of suffering. So it works from inside out. Although it acknowledges all those things in the world outside which make us suffer, it does not start with them. It starts by looking not at what is done to one but what one *does*. It starts by trying to eliminate all those things that one does which *cause* suffering to oneself and others. After all, most of us don't have much control over what goes on in the world outside. But we can control what we ourselves do. So we start with that.

The gateway to the Buddhist Path is the Five Precepts. Anyone who cannot understand these precepts and put them willingly into practice cannot be said to be a practising Buddhist. He will be a Buddhist in name only. Nor can he gain the fruit of Buddhism – Nibbāna.

Buddhism identifies five areas in which we can stop doing things that cause suffering. It codifies them as precepts, which a Buddhist is supposed to keep. They boil down to an undertaking not to cause suffering to oneself and others. The Buddhist path begins with an acceptance of these Five Precepts. With this, the Path to Peace begins.

A Buddhist undertakes to abstain from:

Killing
Stealing
Misuse of the Senses
Lying
Drinks and Drugs, which lead to carelessness

It is obvious that if one sticks to the spirit and letter of these, one will eliminate serious ways in which one is a threat to others and oneself.

By doing this, one takes a stand against suffering and this enables one to see it all the more clearly as it appears in daily life.

Having adopted the Precepts, one's conscience becomes clear and the more immediate problems in everyday life subside, leaving one more peaceful and more clear-sighted.

The three activities which make up one's life, thought, speech and actions, become more obvious and one is in a position to adopt in earnest the detailed method of practice which provides the most efficient and direct route to Nibbāna. This method is the practice of Insight Meditation.

# 4. **THE FIVE BUDDHIST PRECEPTS**

All that we are is the product of what has been done. What we will become is the product of what we are doing now.

Everything is done in the present. The present is like a moving point or wave of activity travelling through time and space.

Although the products of the past are all around us, the past itself has gone. Nothing can be done in the past. As for tomorrow, we can do nothing there until it becomes today.

If we understand this, we see how supremely important it is to do only those things *now* that produce results in the future which are wholly satisfactory. The future is our future. It is we who will inherit the results of our today.

How shall we decide what to do? And what not to do? The best guide is ourselves. We should not do to others what we do not want to be done to us. Since we want to be happy, we should not impair the happiness of others.

It is on this basis that the Five Buddhist Precepts are constructed. These are intentions, promises, which one makes to oneself. They act as a restraining framework within which our activities take place.

*1. I undertake to observe the precept to abstain from killing living beings.*

*2. I undertake to observe the precept to abstain from taking things not given.*

*3. I undertake to observe the precept to abstain from misuse of the senses.*[3]

*4. I undertake to observe the precept to abstain from false speech.*

*5. I undertake to observe the precept to abstain from drinks and drugs causing heedlessness.*

One wants to live. One does not want to die. This is fundamental. Other living beings are the same. They struggle to survive, as any hunter, fisherman, farmer or entomologist knows. In a well-known reading book for very young children it used to say, "Cows give us their milk." They don't. We take it. It is the same with their lives. We take them. Because we want to eat them.

We don't want to be killed ourselves, so we keep the first precept and say that we are not going to kill others.

---

[3] See NOTES on page 79

With stealing it's simple. It causes me inconvenience when someone steals *my* wallet or my car or even my book, so I decide not to steal what belongs to *him.*

Of course you will meet a man who says that, ultimately, nobody can own anything. Philosophically, he may have a point. But the chances are he has his eye on somebody's something. So keep your hands in your pockets.

If you run off with someone else's wife or husband, it causes suffering and often breaks up someone's family as well. If you sleep around without the knowledge of your partner or the other person's partner, it is a breach of trust that can cause a lot of pain. If a relationship doesn't work, it's cleaner just to terminate it. Start again. Without deception.

If you don't refrain from False Speech, if you tell someone something that isn't true, the very least you will cause him is inconvenience.

If we put ourselves in the position of those who are on the receiving end of these actions - who are killed, whose possessions are stolen, who are betrayed by their wives or husbands or sexually abused, who are deceived by the lies and untruths of others, then we will not want to cause that suffering to others.

If we were wholeheartedly to adopt these precepts and live our lives by them, we would no longer cause suffering to other living beings by our actions. In this way we would normalise our relationships with others and the world about us.

Our consciences would become clearer. Although the things that we have done in the past would still cast their shadows on the present, the shadows themselves would fade and we would derive much encouragement from this.

*If these precepts were kept throughout the human world, it would make an unbelievable difference. There would be no war, no serious crime, and no need for money to be spent on armies, policing, courts of justice or prisons.*

## 5. **BUDDHISM AND DRUGS**

As for the Fifth Precept, our society is full of broken lives and human disasters that are the results of alcohol and drug abuse. Crime, road accidents, poverty, broken homes, violence, physical illness, mental illness and misery.

The Fifth Precept is aimed at substances like alcohol, cannabis, opium (and its derivative heroin), cocaine, mescalin, amphetamines, LSD etc. In the Buddha's own time it would have included soma, about which so much is written in Vedic literature.

Why does a Buddhist undertake to abstain from these things? Because they lead to carelessness.

Carelessness leads to mistakes.

Buddhism teaches Karma, cause and effect. If this, then that. If not this, then not that. In dealing with things, Buddhism seeks out the causes. If you change the cause, the effect changes automatically. If, on the other hand, you merely remove the effects and leave the cause untouched, that cause will produce more effects of the same kind. You cut the grass. It grows again. If you want to get rid of it altogether, you have to dig out the roots.

The cause of taking alcohol and drugs is that, when one first experiments with them, one likes what they do to one's body and mind. One feels exhilarated, excited, ecstatic even. One has a feeling of well-being or of greater self-confidence. Or it helps to overcome, or even temporarily disperse altogether, thoughts or memories that are painful or worrying. In short it makes one feel better.

But in the long term it turns out to be more like the bait which ensnares the fish.

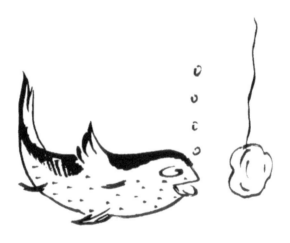

Inside the bait is a hook!

The desirable experiences fade. This makes it necessary to take more. Two pints instead of one. Two pills. Two joints. Still the pleasure diminishes. The doses increase. The pleasure does not. Stronger drugs are needed. Cocaine and opium replace cannabis. Heroin replaces cocaine. LSD replaces amphetamines. Whisky and vodka replace beer.

The decrease in pleasure is accompanied by a corresponding increase in the negative effects. The body becomes increasingly unwell with nausea, pains in the joints and muscles, headaches, fever, loss of appetite, difficulty sleeping, a serious weakening of the immune system. Mentally, there are mood swings from elation to depression, an inability to concentrate, paranoia and loss of memory. At this stage one is drinking and taking drugs not for pleasure, but in order to get a momentary respite from suffering. One is seriously ill.

Inevitably, one's relationships suffer. One finds it difficult to keep a job. Money becomes a serious problem because, as one finds it harder to earn it, the costs of buying alcohol or drugs in the quantities needed for even temporary relief escalate. It is a bleak picture.

Rehabilitation is difficult. Withdrawal symptoms are severe. One hundred percent recovery is uncommon. Often the optimum result is "containment". This means that the patient is kept relatively stable by prescribed "safe" drugs. "Relatively stable" does not mean happy, healthy and enjoying a good life. It means that, while on the medication (which will always have side effects), one is less of a social problem. Quite commonly, there is a relapse. A return to drinking and drug taking. The whole destructive cycle repeats itself. Mind and body are so weakened that serious illness and consequent death are often the result.

It is not only the individual who is affected. The effects on his or her family are devastating. For children, to grow up in a family where there is drink or drug abuse is a terrible start to life.

Of course prevention is better than cure. But it seems clear that the drug education programmes in schools are not entirely successful. Their efforts are not helped by the entertainment artists who target the young. They are often alcoholics and drug takers themselves and contribute to a drug culture in which they are role models. The sad fact is that the entertainment industry makes a lot of money and is very powerful. At the present time, it is not possible for a democratic government to confront the unwholesome propaganda, which targets the young and vulnerable. Assuming that it had the will to do so.

Certainly, in the western democracies, punitive legislation has not worked.

If a water pipe is leaking, the effect is pools of water. If you spend your time mopping up the water with a cloth, you will work for a long time.

To solve the problem you must find the cause of the leak and mend it.

With Buddhism, this simple logical approach is applied to everything. Primarily, it is applied to the fact of suffering. If you wish to escape from suffering you must remove the cause of suffering. If you want to avoid the consequences of alcohol or drug addiction, leave them alone.

Drugs are substances which lead men to carelessness about their own bodies. These become sick and degenerate. Judgement becomes impaired so that men make mistakes in handling their personal affairs, in their work, in their driving and in their relationships with others. If they have families and dependents, these too are affected by the errors of judgement resulting from this carelessness.

The Buddha pinpoints that it is the *carelessness* resulting from taking drugs that results in errors in our thinking and behaviour.

This carelessness is avoided if the *cause,* the drugs themselves, is given up and avoided.

It is worth considering how the type of carelessness that results from drugs works. Drugs dominate a man's mind and body. This causes him to lose the power of sane and rational judgement. As a result of this, he makes mistakes.

It is easy to see, therefore, that 'drugs' that do this do not only grow in the earth as plants or come out of a chemist's laboratory as pills. They can come just as readily from between the covers of a book or a television screen or from the speakers of a radio. As an escape from reality (which is what drink and drug abuse is) books, entertainment and music are widely used. As any schoolboy knows.

For us, the important thing is to apply cause and effect. These things cause suffering to oneself and others. These things I will abstain from. No cause - no effect. No drink and drugs. No carelessness. No consequences.

The relationship of oneself with the world will be re-established in normality. The internal Path can now be trodden with a minimum of interference.

# 6. **THE PRACTICE**

Y et keeping these precepts is the outer shell of morality. It means one is restraining oneself from doing these things.

But if one is restraining oneself, it indicates that there is something to be restrained.

When one investigates this, one can see that before every act of killing, stealing, misuse of the senses, lying and drinking or taking drugs, there is a *mental* impulse to do these things. So long as these mental impulses arise, one cannot be sure that they will never lead to action.

The next step is to purify the mind so that negative or unwholesome states will never arise in us again.

When this is achieved, human beings will have reached the first stage of human completeness or human perfection.

Or, to put it another way, human beings will be back to normal.

This is achieved by Insight Meditation.

Insight Meditation is a form of mental development. It is a kind of meditation that involves looking inside ourselves. Normally our attention is turned outwards towards the world we live in. In this way we gather a lot of information and knowledge about the world. But we often do not know very much about ourselves. Because of this we are unable to free ourselves from suffering and unhappiness.

*The method is to note, with full awareness, everything as it arises, in the present moment, at the sense doors.*

There are six doors of perception:

    The eye for sights
    The ear for sounds
    The nose for smells
    The tongue for tastes
    The sense of touch for physical objects
    The mind for thoughts and states of mind

It is through these six sense doors that we experience the world. Without them we would experience nothing.

The method is simple. But it is not easy. If one can do it, one is face to face with reality itself, the actual continuous flow of one's life. If one perseveres, one comes, by degrees, to understand how everything works; how one's attention is caught by a sense perception and the mind is drawn towards it. How this outward reaching leads to actions through thoughts, feelings, words and deeds that have consequences for oneself and others.

The method is similar to focusing one's attention, minutely, on the detail of the images that appear on the cinema screen. If one can restrain oneself from being drawn into the story of the film, one comes to see that all these pictures, which succeed each other so rapidly, are none of them real; the fire is not hot, the water is not wet, the heroine is not a real girl. Becoming disenchanted with the illusion of it all, suddenly one sees the screen behind it. Similarly, when one becomes disenchanted with the endless flow of phenomena at the sense doors, one has a sudden direct experience of Nibbāna.

The aim of Insight Meditation is the realisation of Nibbāna. Nibbāna is eternal peace and happiness, free from any suffering or unsatisfactoriness. There is nothing higher or better than Nibbāna.

According to this method, when something presents itself to our eyes, we note "seeing". When a sound catches our attention we note "hearing". When our nose responds to a stimulus we note "smelling". When a taste presents itself to the tongue, we note "tasting". When we become aware of physical contact with any object such as our clothes or the floor under our feet, we note "touching". When we experience sensations of discomfort we note them for what they are: "itching", "aching", "stiffness", "tired", "hot", "cold". When thoughts come to our minds we note "thinking".

Obviously, these things are going on all the time but with Insight Meditation, we deliberately direct our attention towards them and try to be aware of them while they are actually occurring. Importantly, we do not make distinctions as to what exactly it is that we see or hear and so on. If we allow ourselves to particularise, we will be drawn into the detail, into trains of thought, and we will lose sight of the general nature of what we experience. As far as the practice goes, it doesn't matter what you are looking at, it all comes down to just "seeing".

Consider a guard at the school gate whose job it is to try to prevent the students from carrying weapons into the school. His job is to see weapons and confiscate them. He doesn't need to particularise; gun, antique sword, razor, garden shears, scissors, nail file, cosh, dagger, mother's kitchen knife, my father's old kukri from India, six-inch nail. The detail doesn't concern him. He is just looking for weapons.

So it is with seeing as just seeing, hearing as hearing, smelling as smelling, tasting as tasting, touching as touching, thinking as thinking. While practising, we try to avoid being drawn into the details and being distracted by the associative thinking which these provoke.

Perceiving things in this way brings about an increasing detachment from the world around us. A centring of ourselves, a new stability.

When we have to move our bodies, we note each movement in two parts. First the intention to move. Then the actual movement itself; "stretching", "bending", "chewing", "reaching", "grasping", etc.

For convenience, the numerous activities that make up our lives from moment to moment are considered to occur in one of four postures:

> Sitting
> Standing
> Walking
> Lying down

When we are practising Insight Meditation, we can adopt any of these four. Meditators who are practising seriously for an extended period of time, usually alternate between a fixed period of sitting meditation and a similar period of walking or standing. Meditating lying down is fine too but there is a tendency to fall asleep. (Sleep is also fine but it doesn't lead to mental development and awareness.)

It is very beneficial to practise last thing at night and first thing in the morning.

Practising like this, we see for ourselves that all activities have two aspects; one is mental, the other physical. In this way, we are introduced to a fundamental principle of Buddhism. This principle appears in the Dhammapada in the Yamakavaggo section:

"Mind comes first."

It is because mind comes first that liberation is possible. If our character and our behaviour were solely conditioned by our physical structure and genetic make- up, there would be no escape for us. We would just be machines. Motorcars can't bring about their own development and become supercars. They need human engineers.

People blame their shortcomings on the fact that "they were born that way", "that's the way they were made", "that's how they were brought up". This then becomes a self-fulfilling prophecy.

They say they cannot change and therefore they don't try. So it seems to be true.

If one is a brunette one may not be able to make oneself a blond without the help of hydrogen peroxide. But if one takes the trouble to investigate why one is a bad man or lazy or angry or violent or untruthful or a smoker or oversexed or shy or timid or arrogant or cruel or many other things that one would rather not be, one will find that all these characteristics arise first in the mind as a series of thoughts. These thoughts in their turn condition speech and behaviour. Repeated continuously, they bring about physical conditions that mirror them.

It is perfectly possible to arrest the flow of these thoughts, to let them go without allowing them to turn into words and actions and, ultimately, to replace them with thoughts and therefore characteristics that one would rather have instead.

One's present character is constructed of the mental building blocks of past thoughts, which continually arise in the present. This is how karma works. One can't change the past but one can learn from it. By working in the present, one can construct the building blocks of one's future character. This is how one uses karma to get what one wants.

But first, theory apart, one needs to see for oneself from moment to moment how it all works. One has to see the workings of mind and body. It is a practical process of continuous investigation, which provides the most amazing insights into life and the process of becoming. The possibilities of self-development are truly endless. Rightly used, they certainly do lead to Nibbāna, the highest happiness, the deathless state.

Of course, Rome wasn't built in a day. How long a journey takes depends on how far away you start from. There are accounts in the suttas of men who completed the journey in less than a day. For others it has taken weeks, months, years or even lifetimes. That is karma again.

But one has to begin somewhere and some time. The method is available. But it is oneself that has to put it into practice now.

Buzz Buzz Buzz
Buzz Buzz Buzz
Buzz Buzz Buzz
Buzz Buzz Buzz
Buzz Buzz Buzz
Buzz Buzz Buzz
Buzz Buzz Buzz
Buzz Buzz Buzz
Buzz Buzz Buzz
Buzz Buzz Buzz

ISN'T IT
PEACEFUL,
DARLING?

# YES

## STOPPING THE MIND

*If stopping were easy,*
*a thought beam*
*properly directed*
*would thread silently*
*through atom after atom*
*and bring the entire universe*
*to a standstill;*
*an empty mirror*
*reflected in itself.*

*If stopping were difficult,*
*the spider mind would jumble on,*
*piling thought on thought,*
*trapped in its own web;*
*the threads spreading out in all directions,*
*the atoms like so many jostling beads*
*dancing and tangling in ever clashing patterns,*
*keeping the entire universe*
*in eternally pulsating chaos;*
*a many-headed monster*
*glaring at its own reflections.*

*Not easy.*
*Not difficult.*
*A judicious response*
*to the Problem of Pain.*

*A letting go*
*of all phenomena.*

*Again.*
                        *(Blondin)*

## THE QUIET MIND

The Sun
(still)
shines
in a bucket of water
but doesn't
get wet.

# 7. **THE METHOD IN DETAIL**

B efore one begins Insight Meditation, it is essential that one both understands and keeps the Five Precepts.

Keeping these precepts normalises one's relations with others by cutting off harmful actions directed towards them. It also gives one a basis for removing the impulses to harm others from one's mind. This is a great help in meditation.

If one is unable to come to terms with and keep these basic precepts it is not possible to come to a realisation of Nibbāna and so one's meditation practice will prove fruitless.

In this case, one would do better to concentrate on activities that help others, particularly the poor and needy. By doing this one acquires merit, which will be of use to one in the future. Helping others whose suffering is greater than our own also purifies the mind.

If we can sincerely accept the Five Precepts, we sit down straight and still, but relaxed. We pay attention to the movement of our abdomen while we are breathing in and out. We note the rising and swelling of the abdomen as we breathe in as "rising". We note the collapse and shrinking of the abdomen as we breathe out as "falling". We make no particular effort to affect the nature of the breathing as to its length or speed. We simply observe and note. "Rising". "Falling". The physical body is the object of this attention. The awareness itself is consciousness, which is a mental activity.

If the mind wanders and thoughts occur, we note them simply as "thinking". We do not follow them up or become distracted by the content of the thoughts. If feelings occur we note them as "feeling". If we experience discomfort we note it as "pain". A noise that distracts us is "hearing". Whatever catches the eye is just "seeing". If nothing catches the attention, we just continue to note the rising and falling of the abdomen.

The more we do this the more peaceful we become. Also we begin to notice where the breathing stops in the abdomen and where it begins again. Where the breathing starts and finishes is the very centre of our being.

Standing and lying down meditation are practised in a similar manner. The attention is directed towards the rising and falling of the abdomen and each movement is noted for what it is. "Rising", "Falling". Just as when we are sitting, anything that presents itself at any of the sense doors is noted for what it is and is not grasped after or followed up.

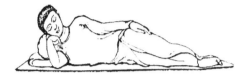

"Seeing". "Hearing". "Tasting". "Smelling". "Touching". "Feeling". "Pain". "Thinking". Et cetera. If the position needs to be adjusted in any way, first the mental act of intention is noted. "Intending". Then the physical movement or sequence of movements. "Lifting". "Stretching". "Reaching". "Scratching". And so on.

Walking is dealt with in a slightly different way. The walking is slow and controlled. The attention is directed to the actual movement of the feet themselves. At first one notes "Left goes thus." "Right goes thus." "Left goes thus." "Right goes thus." When one is familiar with this, one can extend one's awareness so that it can take in the various movements of pressing, lifting, reaching and lowering which make up a complete step.

When one reaches the end of one's walkway one stops and practises standing meditation for a period. Then one notes the intention to turn, notes the various movements which are involved in turning the body round, stands for a while, notes the intention to walk and notes the walking back down the walk-way as before.

This is an outline of a simple and basic method, which allows insight into the nature of things to develop in one's own mind. It is suitable for all, young and old.

If one perseveres, the mind becomes occupied more and more with the here and now and is weaned from its age-old habit of being triggered off into chains of associative thinking. Everything slows down and is more easily observable as the mind becomes concentrated in the present. One is intentionally withdrawing the attention away from the infinite detail of our lives back towards the centre of our being. At this stage, one is withdrawing to the sense doors themselves and watching, carefully, how they operate and how the physical senses interrelate with the mind sense door.

One experiences a new kind of calm and peace, which is not related to, or dependent on, any sense gratification. Therefore, it is accompanied by detachment. Detachment makes it easier to observe the nuts and bolts of living, impersonally; how the senses contact the sense objects and the way the mind rushes out and grasps after them; how this leads to feelings, memories and associative thinking.

One also has a glimpse of a state in which the mind is happy and peaceful and thinking can become a useful tool rather than a mechanistic master.

If one perseveres, one will experience a step-by-step deepening of awareness, which occurs in accordance with natural laws.

Some teachers have classified these steps, and even numbered them. A common classification is one into *Sixteen Steps to Enlightenment*. But these classifications have been made by the mind itself. One has to be careful to avoid getting caught in a mental net of expectation and then thinking the expectations have to be fulfilled.

It's quite possible to go from London to Rome via Paris and Athens but it's not obligatory. The main thing is to get to Rome. Details of a journey are just that; details, mental concepts, thinking. Meditators are not all alike. They have different individual characteristics. The speed at which they develop through the stages varies greatly and depends upon the amount of effort put forth by the meditator and the previous karma of the individual concerned.

No one, however, need lose heart. Nibbāna can be reached by anyone who keeps the Precepts and continues to note patiently each phenomenon as it presents itself at the sense doors. It is difficult for anyone who is accustomed to thinking and distraction to see the profound significance of this Insight Meditation. But it is most important that it be persevered with.

# 8. **THE THREE CHARACTERISTICS**

While practising in this way, one comes to see that all the phenomena that present themselves at the sense doors have certain characteristics in common, irrespective of their details.

The Buddha has classified these characteristics into three:

> All things are impermanent.
> They are without any kind of self.
> They are unsatisfactory.

*IMPERMANENCE*: Everything has a beginning and an end. Things come together, exist for a while and then disappear. They exist not as things in themselves but as collections of other things, which hold together and then fall apart. Nothing endures forever and unchanged.

In the physical world some things seem to last for a long time such as planets and stars; others for a very short time, such as bacteria. But in the end, whatever comes together, falls apart again.

As far as the Practice goes, when we use our senses to evaluate the world around us, this is what we discover from personal experience. We see something for a while, then it vanishes. We hear something, the sound stops. It is the same with the things we smell and touch. It is the same with the mind; thoughts come and go. With the associative mind; one thought triggers off another, that thought yet another. We can think for hours and end up with a thought that seems to have no connection with where we started out and often we can't remember where it started. Even our mental skills, our ability to organise thoughts into useful and meaningful patterns, fade away. We forget. We cannot concentrate. Our aged relatives cannot recognise us. They may not remember their own names.

In practising, we observe all these various phenomena, which present themselves at the six sense doors and we come to the conclusion that everything that happens to us, moment to moment in present time, comes and goes, appears and disappears, is impermanent.

> *Houses go from stone to dust.*
> *The builder is himself undone.*
> *The gate is broken, gone to rust.*
> *Nothing survives from sun to sun.*

> *What was there before the beginning*
> *lingers when stars now born are dead;*
> *in the absence of suns is ever shining,*
> *when nothing is thought and nothing said.*

*NOT SELF:* Everything is without a permanent unchanging self. There are bodies, which are made up of bits and pieces. These come together and fall apart again. The bits are then absorbed by other living beings. Everything in its turn becomes food for something else. If we want to think of our bodies as ourselves, we are free to do so. But we are talking about something that is unlikely to last more than eighty odd years, probably a good deal less.

### CORPSE IN MY ROOM

*An old machine*
*resting there*
*made of bits and pieces*
*whatever happened to be spare*
*of water earth fire and air.*

*An old machine,*
*connected to the mains,*
*switched on, is conscious of its pains.*

*Switched off, inert,*
*it does not know its ending;*
*lies in the dirt,*
*decays and rusts,*
*crumbles to dust,*
*uncomprehending.*

*(Blondin)*

As for our minds, our thoughts and opinions are a continuous changing flux over which we have little control and when we become old our memories fade and sometimes disappear altogether.

> *What of the harvest of that "inner eye"?*
> *Even these mind-made facsimiles*
> *will be lost in old age's imbecilities.*

Body and mind are not ourselves. Nothing in the outside world is ourselves. Other people, nature, objects, houses, cars have their own existences independently of us. We cannot even think of them as our possessions except in a limited conventional sense. We have no ultimate control over them. They belonged to someone else once. They will again.

As far as the practice goes, prolonged observation of mind and body reveals that there is nothing in the nature of a permanent self to be found anywhere in either mind or body. There is just a continuous flux conditioned by karma.

At first this may seem disconcerting. All one's life one has been answering the question "How old are you?" by stating the age of one's body; or responding to comments like "He's intelligent" or "She looks a bit long in the tooth" as though they were made about a real enduring self.

But patient investigation reveals that there is no individual entity to be found anywhere in the flux of phenomena. The nearest one gets to it is the one who appears to be aware or conscious of everything that occurs.

But when that is looked at more closely, it is seen that there is just awareness, just consciousness, which is indistinguishable from the awareness and consciousness found in beings in other forms of nature.

Just as water in a glass is indistinguishable from water in a cup or a kettle. So when the feeling of being disconcerted passes (everything passes), one sees two things; one glimpses that if one could be without the whole flux of mental and physical becoming, one would arrive at an already existing state of peace; one also sees that if there is no fixed unalterable self, we can develop, infinitely improve ourselves and achieve anything.

Using karma; *if this, then that.* In the field of mental development, we plant the seeds, which will produce the plants we want. We can

*"Rise on stepping stones of our dead selves to higher things."* (Tennyson)

*UNSATISFACTORINESS:*   Buddhism   calls   it Suffering.

> "Now this, monks, is the Noble Truth of Suffering: birth is suffering; ageing is suffering; death is suffering; sorrow, lamentation, pain, grief and despair are suffering; association with what we don't love is suffering; separation from what we love is suffering; not getting what one wants is suffering."

In short, life itself, made up of physical and mental experiences, is suffering. Of course, we have always realised that life has its rough and its smooth side. We have taken the rough with the smooth, trying to extend what we like and limit what we don't like. But even the smooth turns out to be rough in the end, for when we get what we want, we experience that it doesn't last or we lose it or it is taken away from us. Or we die away from it. Or we find that *we* change and we no longer want it (all divorces were preceded by marriages).

Life starts with a birth and ends with a death. In between there is an unstable up and down, over which we do not have control. We do not even know that we will wake up tomorrow.

*Ever so long ago. Today.*
*And ever after.*
*Your tears will wash away*
*your broken laughter.*

As one goes on practising, one's own experience confirms the Buddha's teaching; *everything* reveals these three characteristics.

By patient observation, one comes to see that the endless flow of phenomena that presents itself at the sense doors is undesirable. This seeing that something is undesirable causes the desire for it to fade. One's understanding is getting closer to matching one's experience until they equate:

*I see it as undesirable and I do not desire it.*

One turns away from what one no longer desires. One realises that the increasing peace and calm which has been growing inside one as a result of improved concentration and the weakening of the restless, distracted mind, is the gate to Nibbāna itself.

Provided one continues this practice of noting and understanding, irrespective of what phenomena, pleasant or otherwise, may arise, one's progress towards permanent attainment of the Supreme Goal, Nibbāna, is assured. One should never be satisfied with anything less, however enticing it may be, that one meets on the path. Whatever it is, it will always, upon investigation, reveal the three characteristics.

# 9. **THE STAGES OF PROGRESS**

The practice of Insight Meditation takes one further and further back into one's self towards one's ultimate beginning. It is like riding backwards on an elephant. One leaves the point one has reached now by moving out and starts going backwards and inwards to the beginning of it all. Voluntarily.

One experiences some truly remarkable things first- hand, which cause one continually to adjust one's viewpoint. This adjusting and expanding viewpoint gets closer and closer to mirroring how things actually are rather than how one wants them to be.

It is as though one enters a cave leading to the centre of a great mountain from which one emerged a long time ago. One's aim is to reach the centre but one passes so many interesting things, some of which one recognises, and they catch one's attention. How quickly one reaches the centre, depends on the speed at which one moves. The slower one moves the more things one sees to be distracted by. How fast one goes depends on one's concentration, one's determination and the degree of understanding one already has when starting out. In other words on one's previous karma.

So what is one trying to achieve? One is trying to put an end to all suffering. Just that. One continually examines the way in which the mind reaches out towards sense objects because it finds them desirable and how it continually experiences dissatisfaction, either immediately or later. This is the red-hot poker lesson.

One reaches out for the red-hot poker, grasps it and gets burned. Over and over again. Until the repeated pain gives rise to a meaningful Why? How? One investigates, thoroughly and persistently, until at last one sees the whole process. If this, then *that.* If not this*, not that.*

When this is seen, desire spontaneously evaporates. If later one forgets (flesh heals, one forgets), one resumes the process of examination. Over and over and over again until one's understanding, which has been wavering, finally equates to one's experience, which is always the same, and one is free.

*I see it as undesirable and I do not desire it.*

Buddhism teaches that our bondage is due to Ignorance and Compulsive Desire. Ignorance is not knowing, not seeing, not understanding, from moment to moment, the fact of suffering and the cause of suffering. Compulsive Desire translates a Pali word that is usually translated as Craving but really means Thirst. If one thinks of the compulsive thirst of the alcoholic, one is not far off the meaning. The root of craving and thirst is Desire. One desires things that ultimately cause suffering because one finds them desirable. One wants to win so one ends up losing. One wants to drink so one gets a hangover. One smokes dope to get high so one gets addicted. One wants the bait so one gets the hook. One wants to be born so one grows old, gets sick and dies. The moment suffering and understanding balance out, desire on that level evaporates and one is free.

The first stage is reached when one's desire for renewed physical existence wanes. One becomes convinced that the objects of the five physical senses are always ultimately unsatisfactory. They enslave a man without ever giving him the complete and permanent satisfaction that he seeks. To experience them one has to go through the process of birth. When one no longer wants them, one no longer wants to be born. One turns away from physical existence. One will not be born here again.

The second stage is reached when one has the same realisation about the desire for mental existence. Mental states, however refined and exalted, reveal, on investigation, the same three characteristics, though in a much more subtle form. They act as entry points to higher planes of existence, of which there are many. These are more subtle but even more binding. One can no longer say that they are worlds of suffering. They are too subtle, too refined, but they are still certainly unsatisfactory. On the highest plane, the unsatisfactoriness has been reduced to a barely perceptible boredom and an awareness that, even here, things, though they undoubtedly last a long time, do not last forever. They are impermanent like everything else. And when the accrued merit that gives one entry to them has been used up, one falls away to lower levels again.

The final stage is reached when the subtlest desire of all, that for individual existence, is identified as the ultimate bondage which binds us to the wheel of becoming. *If this, then that.* If I want to be something, I will have to lose the something that I become. Everything that has a beginning has an end. For millennia, this urge to be a separate entity, to have a separate consciousness, to be in some way different and individual, has bound us to wandering on from birth to death to rebirth.

Whatever has a beginning has an end. When this is understood and the desire for "I Am" is relinquished there is just an unimaginable and indescribable permanent Peace, which has been here forever.

Permanent? But isn't every thing impermanent? Yes, but *this* state is in no way a *thing*. It has never had a beginning and therefore it has no end. It really has to be experienced for oneself. Thinking cannot reach it.

The Buddha lived and taught for forty-five years after his Enlightenment. A man who has realised Nibbāna doesn't just drop down dead. His body continues the normal ageing process and is vulnerable, as all bodies are, to injury, illness and ultimately death (whatever is born dies). But all the sources of mental suffering have been cut off. There is nothing in which unwholesome states of mind can take root. The craving for future existence is extinct. Peace and happiness are present in the here and now. When the body dies, there will be no more becoming whatsoever.

## HERE

*NOW*
*runs like a crack*
*through the universe.*
*Through it*
*beings escape.*

*Between each step*
*Between each movement*
*Between each breath*
*Between each heartbeat*
*Between each living cell*
*Between each thought*
*Between each impulse*
*Light shines*
*through the crack*
*that runs through*
*the universe NOW.*

*No-one who grasps after*
*even a speck of dust*
*(even his own shadow)*
*can squeeze through this crack.*

*(Blondin)*

# EPILOGUE

There are more books on Buddhism than could possibly be read by one man in his lifetime.

The early Pali suttas represent the most authentic version of the Buddha's actual teachings in his own language. Their publication in the west was pioneered by The Pali Text Society, with the financial support of King Chulalongkorn of Thailand. The texts have all been translated into English.

The PTS still exists and readers can, if they wish, read the suttas for themselves in English (or Pali).

Whether you read or not, get a broad idea of the basic principles and then *practise.* Practice does not depend on literacy.

Many achieved Perfect Liberation from suffering before the Buddha's time and many have achieved it without knowing anything of the Buddha. They did all the work themselves.

Even we, who have a map provided by the Buddha, still have to do the legwork ourselves or we won't complete the journey.

Those who actually want to achieve Perfect Liberation of mind for themselves should remember the story of the hungry man who spent all his time reading menus and starved to death.

The account of the stages of progress may appear to differ from some other accounts. They are based on the author's own experience.

No matter what the label may be,
by its *fruit* we judge the tree.

# APPENDIX

Once there was a Prince who fell in love with a dancing girl. The Chief Minister did not approve of this. However, he knew that he could not oppose the Prince's will directly, so he said,

"What do you like about her?"
*"I like her voice. I like her dancing. I like her skin."*
"Have you looked closely at these things you like about her?"
*"Yes, of course!"*

But the Minister had planted a seed of doubt in the Prince's mind.

He noticed that, when she was singing, it was so beautiful and seemed to come from her very heart. But, in some strange way, it seemed always the same.

So he came very close to her to see how and where she made this beautiful sound. He found that it didn't come exactly from her heart, but from the centre of her chest. He saw a small door and, when he opened it, he discovered a miniature tape recorder. It was from this that the singing came.

He was astonished but he consoled himself by thinking, "At least her dancing is real!" He sat and watched her dancing and he became aware of a faint whirring sound that seemed to be coming from somewhere in her stomach. When he looked, he discovered another small door and behind it an electric motor which made her arms and legs move when she danced.

This was another shock but he thought, "At least her skin is beautiful!" and he took her hand and stroked her arm. Her skin was as smooth and as perfect as it had always been. He sighed. But then something about its smoothness puzzled him. He looked at it very carefully indeed and realised that it was made of plastic. Her whole body was made of plastic!

Just like a doll. That is what she was, a singing, dancing doll.

Of course he no longer loved her. But he felt resentful towards the Chief Minister and took to watching him, looking for some fault that he could use to get him dismissed.

After a while, he noticed that the Minister's voice sounded a little odd, although he had never noticed this before. He also noticed that when he walked, although he held his head up high in a proud way, he walked jerkily like a soldier marching.

The Minister was dressed in fine clothes that covered his whole body. So, of course, the Prince couldn't examine *his* chest and stomach. But one day when he went down to the river to bathe, the Prince followed him. When he took off his fine clothes, the Prince could clearly see that he had two small doors just like the dancing girl. What is more, his skin too looked just like old plastic. But the greatest surprise was that he could see cracks where the different bits of plastic, the arms, the legs and the head, joined onto the body where the two small doors were.

The Minister too was a plastic doll!

Of course by now the Prince found he was looking at everyone in a new way. And whoever he looked at, the King, the Queen, the nobles, the soldiers, the ordinary people – all turned out to be walking, talking plastic dolls.

Some were very crude, some very fine. The ladies painted over the plastic on their faces to make them look more real and even sprayed Eau de Cologne on their joints to disguise the smell of plastic, which the Prince had become more and more aware of.

By now the Prince had become completely dis-enchanted with his life. He could no longer bear to spend his life with a lot of plastic dolls, who creaked and were always trying to wash off the smell of plastic or disguise it with Eau de Cologne.

So he left the palace and went to live in a cave. He used to wander about under the trees, feeling sad until, one day, he felt tired and leaned against a large tree. As soon as his hand touched it, the familiar feel made him realise that it too was plastic. And now he could see quite clearly that it even had plastic leaves.

He went back to his cave and sat slumped against the wall. When he put his hands on his chest and stomach, he had no need to open the two small doors to find out what was behind them. Looking at his hand he could clearly see the crack where it joined onto the plastic wrist. He lay back and did not bother even to close his eyes. And that is where the men sent to find him by the Chief Minister found his plastic body.

But as for the Prince, he had left it behind to go back where he came from.

And the body? Oh they melted it down as they always do and, because he had been a Prince, they wore black armbands for a month and went around trying to look sad.

# NOTES

This is the Third Precept (see page 30):

**Kāmesumicchācārā veramanī sikkhāpadam samādiyāmi.**

*I undertake to refrain from misuse of the senses.*

**Kāmesumicchācārā**, literally and originally, means: *misuse of the senses.* That is, any of the senses. Later, it acquired the more limited meaning of sexual misconduct. This is variously interpreted by different cultures and in different places. Misleadingly, it has acquired the status of a standard English translation.

Of course, it can include adultery and paedophilia. But it is not only misuse of sexual desire. It is misuse of any senses contacting their sense objects and setting up a state of interactive pollution with the mind.

Think of those Roman gluttons who, having eaten as much as they could, vomited it all up and returned for more! Think of youngsters with earphones on full blast to shut out the world. Think of Cleopatra and her vials of perfume and daily baths in fresh asses' milk. Think of drunkenness, drug addiction, body piercing, masochism. Think of uncontrolled thinking.

*MAY ALL BEINGS BE HAPPY*
*MAY THEY BE FREE FROM ILL WILL*
*MAY THEY BE FREE FROM ENMITY*
*MAY THEY BE WELL AND HAPPY ALL THE TIME*
*AND MAY THEY ALL REACH NIBBĀNA*

9 780957 190139